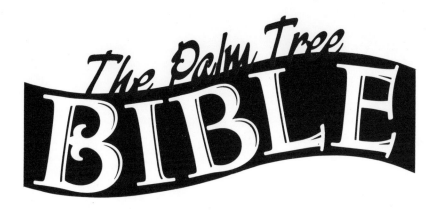

The Palm Tree BIBLE

The Favorite Stories of God and His People from the Old Testament

BOOK THREE

DAYBREAK PUBLISHERS

P.O. Box 261129 • San Diego, CA 92196

DB46203
ISBN 1-885358-19-9

BOOK THREE

Stories from Scripture
retold by
RACHEL HALL

LORNA LEWIS

UNA McKENNA

BARBARA McMEEKIN

JANE PORTER

SUSAN SAYERS

KATHY SINGLETON

KATHIE SMITH

Illustrated by
ARTHUR BAKER

THE PALM TREE BIBLE
© 1996 Palm Tree Press

Published in the United States of America by
DAYBREAK PUBLISHERS
P.O. Box 261129 • San Diego, CA 92196

Printed in Hong Kong

Contents

God Makes the World

God made the sun, the moon,
the stars and all the mountains,
rivers and seas. Then He made
all the animals, and
people as well.

In the beginning
there was nothing at all;
like when you
shut your eyes tight
and cover your ears.

It was dark
and empty
and silent
and still.

But God had a
very good idea.

"Let there be light!"
He said.

And there it was,
bright and golden.

He split the light
and darkness
to make day time
and night time.

And that was the very first day.

The next day God said,
"Let the waters and the sky
be split up, too."

And, just as He wanted,
it happened.

A huge blue sky
looked down on
a huge blue sea.

"Now," said God,
"Let all the waters
run together
into one place,
so there is
some dry land."

With a gush
and a rush

and a splash
and a trickle

the waters moved;
and there was the land!

God was very pleased.

"I will make plants
to grow on this land,"
said God.

And the plants
began to grow.

There was grass,
there were trees,
there were hundreds
of flowers:
red and yellow,
purple and pink,
orange and white and blue.

"and a softer light
  for night time,"
  God went on.

(That was the moon, of course.)

He made all the twinkling stars,
  as well.

So now there could be
  seasons for all the plants
  to grow in —
  Spring,
    Summer,
      Fall and
        Winter.

"This is very good,"
  said God, happily.

"I will make birds, now,
  to fly in My sky;
  and swarms of sea creatures
  to swim in all the water."

There were apples and oranges,
  pears and bananas,
  pineapples, walnuts,
  strawberries and grapes.

God was really enjoying Himself!

After that He said,
  "Let there be a great light
  to shine in the sky
  in the daytime."

Can you guess what it was?

Yes — the sun!

Sure enough,
  the waters began to
  wiggle and squirm with life:
  tadpoles and shrimp,
  jellyfish, crabs and oysters,
  cod, salmon and eels.

Can you think of any more?

Well, God made them, too!

And overhead,
  all the colorful birds
  swooped and glided,
  singing in the sunlit sky.

"Cheep, cheep!"
  "Caw, caw!"
"Hoot, hoot!"
  "Tweet, Tweet!"

God was delighted.
  "It's just as good
  as I hoped!" He said.

"There must be animals
   to live on the land, too,"
   said God,
   "lots of different kinds."

He made
   creepy-crawly ones,
   slithery-slimy ones,
   scuffling, hopping
   and jumping ones;

He made
   some which climbed
   and swung through His trees,
   and some which quietly grazed
   on His grass.

Some could run
   as fast as the wind,
   while others could hardly
   move at all.

"Now we are ready
   for the best part of all,"
   said God.

"I will make some creatures
   that are like Me,
   and I will put them in charge
   of everything I have made."

So God made people,
   both men and women,
   to live in His beautiful world.

"Have lots of children,"
   God told them.
   "I want people to live
   all over My world.

"Do you see My fish
   and My birds?
Do you see My forests
   and My lions?

God made bigger creatures
   to live in the deep oceans —
   there, the sharks could swim,
   dolphins could play,
   and great whales
   could wallow
   and dive.

"Have lots of children,"
   God told them.

"There's plenty of room
   for you all
   in My world."

God looked around
  at the world
  He had made.
  Though He had been so busy,
  He was very happy.

What a good idea
  it had been!

That day on earth,
  bees buzzed lazily,
  panthers dozed in the sun;
  and God rested
  after all His work.

Note:
This story can be found
in Genesis 1:1 – 2:3.

"Well, I want you
  to look after them all.
  I have made plenty
  of fruit and plants
  for you all to eat."

Noah's Big Boat

Noah trusted God, but a lot of other people didn't. So God helped to save Noah and his family when the earth was flooded.

But the rest of the people
  were very wicked
  and did not listen to God.

They were always fighting
  and arguing
  and being nasty.

They stole each other's sheep
  and cattle and bread.
  Nothing was safe.

In fact,
  they were all quite horrible!

It made God very sad.
  They were spoiling
  the beautiful world
  He had made.

So God decided
  to send a flood of water
  to cover the whole earth.

Noah was a farmer.

He lived on his farm
  with his wife and three sons:
  Shem, Ham and Japheth.

The sons married
  and brought their wives
  to live on the farm, too.

They were a happy family
  who loved and served God.
  Noah trusted God in all things.

God spoke to Noah:
  "Noah, I want you
  to build a very big boat."

"That's funny," thought Noah,
  and scratched his head,
  "there's no lake or ocean nearby!"

"Noah," said God, "build
  a boat big enough to hold
  all your family
  and two of every kind
  of animal and bird.
  I am sending a flood
  but I will keep you safe."

"Strange," thought Noah,
  "we don't get much rain
  around here!"

But he knew he could trust God,
  so he started to work.

Noah and his sons
  chopped down trees.
  "T-i-m-b-e-r-r-r," they yelled.

They worked
  from morning until night,
  chopping, sawing and hammering.

Their neighbors came and
  watched.
  "They're crazy," they said,
  and they laughed and laughed
  until their sides ached!

Why, whoever thought
  it would rain so much
  that all the earth
  would be covered?

At last the boat was ready.

Then God said:
  "Noah, load the boat
  with lots of food
  and round up the animals."

So Noah and his family
  got the animals in, two by two.

Among the many animals were:
  Mr. and Mrs. Tigger, the tigers;
  Gertie and George, the giraffes;
  Katie and Karl, the kangaroos;
  Mr. and Mrs. Hippo, the
  hippopotami;
  Micky and Mindy, the monkeys;
not forgetting:
  Mr. and Mrs. Woolley, the sheep;
  Harold and Henrietta, the
  hamsters;
  Doris and David, the doves;
  Sid and Sarah, the snakes; and
  Mr. and Mrs. Plodalong, the
  turtles, who were always last.

When everyone was inside,
  God closed the big door tight
  so that no water could get in.
  Then those in the ark waited
  and waited and waited.
They waited for seven days,
  and then the first drops
  of rain fell — pit-ter, pat-ter,
  pit-ter, pat-ter.
The rain fell faster and faster
  and harder and harder —
  pitter-patter, pitter-patter,
  pitter-patter, pitter-patter.
The rivers began to rise
  and burst their banks.
The seas were raging storms.
The towns were flooded
  and the people were scared.

They wished they had
  listened to God now.
Soon, even the trees
  and mountains
  were covered by water.
  And still it rained —
  pitter-patter, pitter-patter.
For 40 days
  and 40 nights
  it rained.

And Noah's boat floated safely.

Inside, Noah and his family
  were kept busy
  feeding the animals
  and cleaning out their cages.
There was something to do
  all the time:
Micky and Mindy, the monkeys,
  were always
  up to some mischief.

Poor Gertie and George,
  the giraffes,
  kept bumping their heads!

And Noah had to watch
  that Mrs. Hippo didn't sit on
  little Harold and Henrietta,
  the hamsters!

At last, the rain stopped.

God sent a wind to blow
  and the water began to go down.

The boat came to rest
  on the top of a mountain.

Noah looked out.
All he could see
  was water
  and more water.

He sent Rita, the raven,
  to look for land
  but she could not find any,
  and just flew
  around and around.

After seven days
  Noah sent Doris, the dove,
  to look for land.
  But she could not find any either,
  so she came back to the boat.

"Oh, dear," thought Noah,
  "it is taking a long time
  for the water to go down."

Seven days later,
  Noah sent Doris out again.
  This time, she came back
  with an olive leaf in her beak
  to build a nest!

"Hurrah!" shouted everyone.
  "The water is going down!"

Another seven days passed
  and Noah sent Doris out again.
  This time
  she did not come back.
  She had found a place to nest!

Everyone was so excited!
  They couldn't wait
  to get their feet
  on dry land again.

Micky and Mindy wanted
  to swing through the trees;
Sid and Sarah longed
  to slither over the hot stones;
  and Mrs. Hippo dreamed
  of her dream-home in the jungle
  with lots of baby hippos
  running around!

Even Mr. and Mrs. Plodalong,
  the turtles,
  seemed in a hurry!

A few weeks went by
  before the land
  was dry enough to stand on.
  Then God told Noah
  to lower the door.

A great shout of joy went up!
The animals
  leaped, ran, jumped,
  slithered
  or just plodded down
  the gang plank,
  two by two.

They said good-bye
  to Noah and his family,
  and went off
  to make their new homes
  and raise their own families.
  And Mrs. Noah
  shed a tear or two.

Noah was glad he had trusted God
  and obeyed Him.

He and his family thanked God
  for saving them.

Then they set about
  building new homes
  and planting
  new crops.

And God promised
  Noah and his family
  He would never again
  send such a big flood.

And He put a rainbow
  in the sky
  as a sign of His promise.

Note:
This story can be found
in Genesis 6:9 – 9:17.

16

Joseph the Dreamer

Joseph was one of Jacob's 12 sons. In fact, he was his favorite son, and this made Joseph's brothers jealous, so they sold him as a slave.

This is the story of Joseph,
  who lived in a land called
  Canaan.

Would you believe
  he had 11 brothers?

Ten were older than him,
  and just one was younger.

The oldest was named Reuben,
  and the youngest
  was named Benjamin.

Their father was named Jacob.

Every day Jacob would gather
  his 12 sons around him
  and talk to them about God.

Everyone in this large family
  had to work very hard
  because there were so many
  mouths to feed.

The older brothers
  worked in the fields,
  looking after their father's sheep.

When Joseph was 17,
  he began to go along
  to the fields with his brothers.

He wanted to help, too.

But his brothers
  were not too happy about that.

"Oh, no!"
  they would moan to each other.
  "Do we have to take Joseph
  along?"

You see,
  Joseph was his father's favorite
  son, and the others were jealous.

Jacob loved Joseph so much
  that he gave him a special coat.

It was made of lots of small pieces,
  all stitched together,
  and it had beautiful long sleeves.

When the brothers
  saw this beautiful coat,
  you can imagine
  how they grumbled
  and groaned among themselves.

"Why does Dad
  make such a fuss over him?"
  asked one.

"We could all use
  a nice new coat,"
  another said.

"It doesn't suit him anyway!"
  said a third, jealously.

The brothers were all very angry!

Now one night
  Joseph had a dream.

In the morning
  he jumped out of bed
  and rushed to tell his brothers.

"Listen!" he said.
 "We were all in a field,
 tying up bundles of corn.
 Then my bundle stood
 in the middle
 and yours bowed down to mine!"

This made the brothers very angry.

"Does that mean you think
 you are more important
 than we are?"
 they shouted.

Poor Joseph!

His brothers didn't like him,
 and they didn't want
 to talk to him anymore
 — especially when he announced
 that he had had another dream.

"This time," he said,
 "the sun, moon and 11 stars
 were bowing down to me!"

Joseph's brothers
 became very fed up with him
 and his dreams!

One day
 Jacob said to Joseph:
 "Your brothers are out looking
 after the sheep.
 Go and see how they are doing,
 will you?"

It was a long, dusty walk,
 but after a while
 Joseph saw his brothers
 in the distance.

But his brothers
 had seen him first.

"Here comes the dreamer,"
 they said.

"He's probably only come
 to spy on us
 and tell Father what we are doing.
 Let's kill him
 and throw him into this pit.
 Then we can tell Father
 a wild beast caught him."

While they were eating,
  they saw some traders
  coming toward them.

The traders' camels
  were piled high with goods
  for sale in the markets of Egypt.

"Hey!" said Judah.
  "We don't really want
  to kill Joseph, do we?
  Why don't we sell him
  to these men?"

"Good idea!" cried the brothers.

So…
  when the traders came close,
  the brothers took poor Joseph
  from the pit.

Instead of rescuing him,
  they sold him to the traders.

Twenty pieces of silver
  was the price they got!

And so the wicked brothers plotted!

But Reuben, the oldest brother,
  knew how much
  his father loved Joseph.

"No! Don't kill him," he said.
  "We'll just throw him
  into the pit."

So when Joseph arrived,
  the wicked brothers
  tore off his coat
  and threw him into the pit.

"Now we're rid of him!"
  they cried,
  and off they went
  to have their lunch.

So when Reuben
  went back to the pit,
  Joseph was nowhere to be seen.

"Oh no!" Reuben gasped,
  "What shall I do?"

He called all the brothers together,
  and they hatched a plot.

They would tell their father
  a lie.

This is what they did:

They caught hold of a goat
  and killed it.

Then they dipped
  Joseph's lovely coat
  in the blood.

They showed their father
  the coat and said,
  "Look!
  A wild animal attacked Joseph
  and killed him!"

And, of course,
  when Jacob heard
  the brothers' story,
  he just sat down on his bed
  and cried
  and cried
  and cried.

In the meantime,
  the traders had taken Joseph
  to Egypt
  and sold him as a slave.

The man who bought him
  was named Potiphar,
  and he was a captain
  in the king's army.

"That boy looks good and strong,"
  Potiphar thought to himself.
  "I'll put him to work
  in my house."

And Potiphar was right!
  Not only was Joseph strong,
  but he worked hard as well.

Potiphar was very pleased,
  and put Joseph in charge
  of his house
  and all the servants.

Neither had God forgotten Joseph.
  In His own time
  God would release Joseph
  from slavery
  and call him to do great things.

But that is another story.

Note:
This story is found
in Genesis, chapter 37.

21

Joseph Helps His Brothers

After a lot of difficulties, Joseph becomes a friend of the king of Egypt. He helps the king to feed hungry people — including Joseph's own brothers.

Joseph was alone
  in the kitchen one day.
  His master, Potiphar, was
  holding a big party that evening.

Had they gotten enough figs?
  Enough wine?
  Enough bread?
  Enough meat?

Joseph wanted everything
  to be just right.
  In came Alicia.
  She was Potiphar's wife.

Alicia was very pretty.
  She had wide, dark eyes
  and silky black hair.
  That morning she was wearing
  her best white robe and
  a belt sparkling with jewels.

Now Alicia thought Joseph
  was very handsome.
  Even though
  she was married to Potiphar,
  she wanted Joseph
  to cuddle with her.

Oh, dear!

Joseph didn't want to!
  He knew this was wrong.
  Potiphar would be angry.
  What's more, God wouldn't
  be at all pleased.

So Joseph ran off.

It wasn't his day.

He left his robe behind.

When Potiphar came home,
  Alicia showed him Joseph's robe.
  She told him some
  bad stories about Joseph.

Potiphar was so angry!
  He threw Joseph into
  prison right away.

Until one day, he was brought out,
  cleaned up,
  and taken before the
  king of Egypt!

What a nasty place it was!
  Dark, damp, drafty, smelly
  — even a rat or two!

Joseph was very sad.
  He hadn't done anything wrong.
  And he stayed in the prison
  a long time.

The king was feeling worried.
  "Can you help me out?"
  he asked.
  "I've had these curious dreams,
  and I can't understand
  what they mean.
  My wine steward says you
  told him what his dreams
  meant when he was in prison.

"I dreamed there were seven cows —
  big fat ones — eating the grass
  on the riverbank,"
  the king continued.
  "Along came seven thin cows.
  Would you believe
  they ate the seven fat cows?
  And they still looked just as thin!

"I also dreamed that
  seven big ears of corn,
  all on one stalk,
  were swallowed up by
  seven small thin grains."

Now Joseph was a bit of
  a dreamer himself.
  That was one reason why
  his brothers hadn't liked him,
  and had sold him as a slave.

He thought carefully.

"For seven years, your majesty,
   there will be big harvests and
   plenty of everything to eat.
   After that will come
   seven years of famine.
   It will be so bad that
   you'll forget all about
   the good times."

The king and all his advisers
   felt very sad.

"I suggest," said Joseph,
   "that you put someone
   in charge who can prepare
   the country right away.
   There isn't a moment to lose."

The king made his mind up quickly.
   "God has shown you all this,
   so you must be more clever and
   wise than anyone else.
   I think you're just the man
   for the job.
   It's up to you, Joseph."

So Joseph became governor
   of Egypt.
   He was more important than
   anyone else, except the king!

The next seven years were the
   busiest in his life.
   The harvests were so good that
   there was plenty to spare.
   He made sure that
   as much corn as possible
   was gathered into special store
   houses all over Egypt.

Then the famine came,
   just as Joseph had said.
   The Egyptians were all right —
   Joseph had seen to that.

But over in Canaan,
   Joseph's brothers
   and his father Jacob
   got really hungry.

So off they went.
  All except Benjamin.

It was a long, dry, dusty journey.
  But at last they got to Egypt.
  They went to see
  the person who was in charge.
  Of course, that was Joseph.
  Joseph was a bit older now
  and he wore Egyptian clothes.
  The brothers didn't recognize him.

But Joseph knew at once
  who they were.

He decided not to tell them
  just yet who he was.
  He had a strange plan
  to help the brothers he loved.

"You're spies, aren't you?
  Out to do mischief.
  Well, you can have your corn,
  but I will keep one of you here.
  If you want him back, you'll have
  to bring your other brother,
  whom I know you left behind.
  He will tell me if you're honest."

"We can't just sit and
  starve," said Jacob.
  "You had better go to Egypt.
  I hear they have corn there."

"I'm your brother Joseph, whom
you sold into Egypt."

They were surprised!

"Don't worry," said Joseph.
"It was really God who sent
me here, to save people's
lives in this famine.
I will take care of you.
You must live here in Egypt
with me."

And so they did.
Their father Jacob came, too,
and all their families.

They were all together again
once more.

Thanks to Joseph!

Note:
This story is found
in Genesis, chapters 39-46.

Old Jacob couldn't believe it
when the brothers came back
without Simeon.
First Joseph, then Simeon —
he'd lost two sons!

But the famine got worse
and worse.
Soon there was nothing
to eat at all.

So back the brothers went to Egypt.
Jacob didn't like it, but
this time they took Benjamin.

Joseph was so glad to see Benjamin
and all his brothers again.
Soon he told them who he was.

Baby in a Basket

Baby Moses was hidden in a basket by his mother because King Pharaoh wanted to kill him. The princess found him and looked after him.

A long, long time ago
  God's special people,
  the Hebrews,
  were free and happy.

There were lots and lots of them,
  men,
  women
  and children,
  and they all lived in a land
  called Egypt.

They had farms, shops
  and lovely homes.

Then one day
  Egypt had a new king
  — King Pharaoh.

He didn't like the Hebrews at all
  and he decided he would make
  slaves of them.

So this wicked king made life very
  difficult for the Hebrews.

He started by making them build
  huge sheds where he could store
  all the grain that was grown in
  his kingdom.

But the funny thing was
  the more King Pharaoh
  tried to destroy the Hebrews,
  the more their numbers grew
  and grew
  and grew,
  until there were so many of them
  that he got really frightened.

"They'll take over my kingdom,"
  he cried.
  "What shall I do?"

So what do you think the king did?

He made things worse.
  Not only did he force
  the Hebrews to build the huge sheds
  — he also made them make mud bricks
  with straw in them. Then he even
  made them search for the straw
  to put in the bricks.

That was a really nasty job!

But even this did not stop
  the Hebrews from having
  more and more children.

"I'll fix them," thought the wicked
  King Pharaoh.
  "I'll give orders to kill all the
  newborn boy babies.
  We'll throw them into
  the river."

What a terrible man he was!

28

Living near the king's palace
  was a Hebrew family
  — Amram, his wife, Jochebed,
  their son, Aaron, and Miriam,
  their daughter.

Jochebed was expecting
  another baby
  when the king gave his order
  to kill all the newborn boys.

Amram and Jochebed
  were so worried.

And, horror of horrors,
  the new baby was a boy.

But the day came when Jochebed
  could no longer hide the baby.

She would soon be found out.
  So,
  she made a beautiful basket
  for her baby and
  laid it among the bulrushes
  at the side of the river.

Jochebed told her daughter,
  Miriam,
  to stand a little way off
  and watch what happened
  to the baby.

And this is what Miriam saw.

Knowing that King Pharaoh would
  have her baby thrown
  into the river,
  Jochebed went to great lengths
  to hide the baby.

She thought of all sorts of places
  to put him
  — in a cupboard,
  — under the bed,
  — in the laundry,
  — even in a tree trunk!

29

That morning,
  King Pharaoh's beautiful
  daughter had decided to
  bathe in the river.

Just at that moment
  Miriam, who had been
  watching all the time,
  came up to the princess.

"Shall I find a Hebrew woman
  to nurse the baby, Princess
  Fatima?" she asked.

So Princess Fatima left the palace
  with her servants
  and they all made their way
  to a quiet spot.
  The princess knew she would
  not be disturbed there.

And it just happened to be
  the exact spot where Jochebed
  had left her baby in the basket.
  Princess Fatima saw the basket
  and looked inside.

"What a beautiful baby," she said.
  "He must belong to a Hebrew."

"Yes, please," the princess replied.
  "That is a very good idea."

So,
  as quick as lightning,
  Miriam went to get her mother.

Jochebed was so happy
  when Miriam told her
  what had happened.

She ran all the way
  to the river.

When Moses was older
he went to live
at the palace
with Princess Fatima.
She treated him like a son
and even the wicked king
was kind to him.

But Moses knew he was a Hebrew.
He knew that his own people
were slaves to the king.
He knew that was wrong.

But Moses did not know yet
that God had chosen him
to be the leader of the Hebrews.

God was not quite ready
to free His own people yet.

Just give Moses a few more years
to grow into a fine strong man,
God thought to Himself,
then he will lead the
Hebrews — My special people —
to freedom in the Promised Land.

When she got there
Princess Fatima said to Jochebed:
"Please look after this little baby
for me. I will pay you well
for your work."

So Jochebed got her baby back
and, of course,
Princess Fatima made sure
he was safe from King Pharaoh.

And the princess decided to call
the baby Moses, a name that
means "taken from the water."

Note:
This story is found
in Exodus 1:1 – 2:10.

Escape Through the Sea

The Egyptians were cruel to the Israelites and treated them as slaves. Then God chose Moses to lead the Israelites out of Egypt.

Their masters were the Egyptians,
  who were cruel to them
  and made them work
  from morning to night,
  making bricks, bricks,
  and more bricks.

What a nasty job!

But God
  loved the Israelites very much,
  and God had had enough of this!

He decided to free the Israelites
  from slavery
  and take them to a country
  they could call their own
  — a Promised Land!

God needed someone
  to lead His people.

He chose Moses, a fine man
  — he was just right for the job,
  God decided.

"Moses!" God said,
  "You are to go to Pharaoh,
  the king of the Egyptians,
  and demand freedom
  for the Israelites."

Drudge,
  drudge,
  drudge,
  — that was the life
  the Israelites led.

They were slaves
  — for over 400 years
  the Israelites had been slaves.

So, just to persuade them
  to let the Israelites leave,
  He made life uncomfortable
  for them.

He covered the country with frogs;
  He sent terrible hailstorms;
  then there were millions
  of flies everywhere;
  everybody came down with boils;
  and some other
  really bad things happened.

While all this was happening
  to the Egyptians,
  the Israelites were having
  a big celebration in God's honor.
  It was called
  the feast of Passover.*

There was special food.
Everyone prayed to God
  and thanked Him
  for His goodness.

*It is called "Passover" because God "passed over"
His people when He sent the worst trouble.

Moses took a bit of persuading,
  but eventually,
  taking his brother Aaron along,
  he went to see King Pharaoh.

But the king was in no mood to let
  the Israelites leave Egypt.

They were too valuable
  — after all,
  who would do all the work
  if they left?

He threw Moses and Aaron
  out of his palace.

Then he made things even
  worse for the Israelites
  — he made them work
  twice as hard!

Well, of course,
  God got rather mad
  at the Egyptians.

Off they went!
  About 600,000 men
  and their wives and children
  as well.
  Then there were the animals
  — too many of those to count.

The Israelites were so happy.

"At last we are free!"
  they told each other.

"At last we will live
  in our own country!"

"At last we can worship our God
  without fear!"

And God guided them
  on their journey.

During the day
  He went in front of them
  as a pillar of cloud.

At night
  — so that they could see Him —
  He went as a pillar of fire.

God led the Israelites
  through the desert.

Day after day
  they marched,
  through the dust and dirt,
  through sandstorms,
  and at night
  they had to brave the cold.

At last
  God brought them to the Red Sea,
  and the Israelites set up camp
  on the shore.

God had told the Israelites
  that they must be ready
  to leave Egypt
  at a moment's notice,
  so they were all dressed
  in their traveling clothes.

At last,
  King Pharaoh decided
  that life might be easier
  if he let the Israelites go.

He called Moses and Aaron
  back to the palace
  and said to them:
  "Take all your people
  out of Egypt
  and leave us alone.
  Take all your sheep and cows
  and go.
  You will be free
  to worship your God
  — and while you are at it,
  say a prayer for me."

Back in Egypt, King Pharaoh
  was having second thoughts!

He and the rest of the Egyptians
  were missing the Israelites:
  there was no one
  to do the cooking;
  no one to clean the houses;
  no one to repair the roads;
  no one to do all the hard work.

"Let's get them back!"
  the king shouted.

"Call out the army!
  Get the chariots ready!
  We're going after them!"

Just imagine
  how the Israelites felt
  when they saw Pharaoh's army
  charging toward them!

Terrified!

They turned on Moses.
  "We thought
  you would lead us to freedom.
  Instead we shall die
  in the desert!"

Moses was firm with them.
  "Don't be afraid," he said.
  "Pray to God,
  and He will look after you."

And, of course,
  God did look after
  the Israelites.

God said to Moses:
  "Take hold of your stick,
  and stretch out your hand
  over the sea."

The Israelites could hardly believe
  what happened next.

Before their eyes
  was a wide pathway
  through the sea
  — an escape route
  from the Egyptians.

The Israelites marched on
  fearlessly.

On each side of the pathway
  there was a high wall of water.

But they were safe
  — God would see to that.

God had saved His people,
  and they were quick
  to thank Him.

They prayed,
  and sang this song to Him:
  "God looked after us;
  He has defeated our enemies.
  There is no one
  as great as our God.
  God will show us
  the way to a country
  where we can praise Him.
  God is our King forever!"

Note:
This story is found
in Exodus, chapters 4-15.

As soon as King Pharaoh
  realized what had happened,
  he ordered his men to give chase.

The whole Egyptian army galloped
  into the pathway
  between the waters.

Seeing this,
  God told Moses
  to stretch his hand out
  over the sea again.

Immediately, the pathway
  disappeared
  — and so did
  the entire Egyptian army!

Food in the Desert

Moses led the people of Israel out of Egypt. As they walked through the desert, they became very hungry, so God sent them some special food to eat.

God had promised them
  a land of their own,
  with lush green grass
  for their cows to eat,
  and lovely flowers where bees
  could gather nectar.

There would be plenty of milk
  and plenty of honey —
  lots of food
  for everyone.

But,
  before they could reach that land,
  they had to travel through
  a very dry, very dusty
  and very large desert.

It took them many years,
  and they didn't enjoy it much.

First of all,
  they got terribly thirsty.
  That started them all grumbling.

"This is even worse than
  making bricks in Egypt!"
  muttered Zeb.

"At least we could have
  a drink there,"
  grumbled Maleah.

"Makes me wonder why Moses
  bothered to bring us here
  in the first place,"
  mumbled Jess,
  kicking the dust.

Moses had brought
  the people of Israel
  out of Egypt
  where they had been slaves.

Now they were free,
  but they still had
  a very long way to go.

Moses came staggering up
  carrying a large branch of a tree.
  He was quite out of breath.

"God has told me how to make
  it taste better," he puffed,
  and threw the branch
  into the water.

They all watched
  while Ted tried to drink again.
  This time he went on drinking,
  so everyone else joined in.

The water was cool and refreshing.
  They began to think the desert
  was not so bad after all.

"Thanks, Moses," they said.

Moses grinned.
  "Remember, it's God
  you've got to thank!"
  he answered.

Just then, they noticed
  a lake not far away.

"Water!" shouted everyone.
  And they ran to drink it.

Young Ted got there first.

But you should have
  seen his face
  when he took a gulp.

"Ugh! It tastes awful!"
  he said,
  spitting it out
  as quickly as he could.

Later on, the people gathered up
  their children,
  their cattle,
  their sheep,
  and their goats,
  and started off again.

As they walked, they chattered
  and sang songs,
  and every night
  they set up camp
  and rested.

Every morning they packed up
  their belongings
  and continued to walk.

After some time they began
  to run out of food.

Of course, there was nowhere
  in the desert to get any more!

The grumbling started again.
  "It's all Moses' fault!"

"If he had left us in Egypt,
  we would be having meat stew
  for dinner tonight."

"Yes, and as much bread
  as we liked."

They were so hungry
  and so angry with Moses
  that they forgot
  to trust God to provide
  them with food.

But Moses didn't forget.

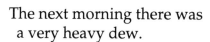

He went off on his own
  and prayed:
    "Lord, what on earth
    shall I do now with
    these people of Yours?"
  he asked.

"They are so fed up
  with being hungry
  that they will be throwing
  stones at me next."

"Don't worry!" God told Moses.

"I will give them meat
  and bread
  so they won't starve.
  You'll see!"

That evening a flock of quail
  flew over the camp.

The birds were on their way
  to another country,
  and some of them
  were so weak and tired
  that they dropped down
  to the ground nearby.

The hungry Israelites
  were able to use them
  to cook a good, tasty supper.

It was delicious!

The next morning there was
  a very heavy dew.

Pete and Beth were up early
  watching lizards play
  in the dusty soil,
  so they were the first
  to see what the dew left behind.

There were thin white flakes
  all over the ground.

They took some back to the camp.

"What is it?"
  asked Pete's mother.

No one knew what it was.

"Let's show it to Moses,"
  suggested Beth.
  "He'll know."

Moses peered
  at the white flaky stuff.

Then he sniffed it
  and looked very happy.

"There you are, you see,"
  he said at last.
  "I told you God
  would look after us.
  He gave you meat for dinner
  last night, didn't He?"

"Well, now He has sent
  you this for breakfast."

The people decided to call it
  "manna,"
  and they liked it very much.

It tasted like honey.

Moses called everyone together
  and gave them God's
  instructions.

"Now, each morning you must
  collect as much manna
  as you can eat in one day,"
  he told them.
  "But don't be greedy!
  And don't keep any for
  the next day, either."

"God won't let you down —
  there will be
  a fresh supply each day."

Everybody took a bowl of some sort
  and set off to work.

Little Nicole toddled about
  filling her tiny bowl.

Big Jake sat on the ground
  and filled his huge bowl.
  It needed to be big!

And all through the day everyone
  had just the right amount to eat.

"Three cheers for Moses!"
  they called,
  licking their fingers.

Moses waved and smiled as he ate
  from his middle-sized bowl.

"Three cheers for God, you mean,"
  he reminded them.

But not everyone was so sure
  that God could be trusted.

Neil and his brothers decided
  it would be much safer
  to store some extra manna
  overnight, just in case.

The next morning there was
  a rather nasty smell
  around their tent.

The manna had gone all moldy
  and it was full of worms!

Moses was very angry.
  "I told you that God promised
  to provide enough food
  each day!"
  he shouted.

"Why did you keep some
  from yesterday,
  for goodness sake?"

Neil and his brothers
  hung their heads.

"We're sorry, Moses," they said.
  "But it's hard to trust
  that your food will just happen
  to be there every day."

Moses agreed that it wasn't easy.

"That's why God told us
  to collect the food each day.
  He is teaching us to trust Him,"
  he explained.

And sure enough,
  God could be trusted.

He provided manna for
  every family, every day,
  so that no one
  had to go hungry.

Note:
This story is found
in Exodus 15:22 – 16:36.

Samson, the Super-Strong

Samson was a very strong man.
The Philistines hated him, and
were always looking for ways to
make him weak.

Manoah and his wife
  lived on a lovely farm,
  but they had no child
  to run around in it.

Until one day a messenger came
  from God.

He told them they would have a son
  quite soon.

"Don't drink any wine,"
  he told Jessica.
  "And let the boy's hair
  grow long.
  That will be a sign
  to everyone
  that he belongs to God."

Sure enough,
  Manoah and Jessica
  did have a child.

He was surprisingly strong!

Sometimes he watched
  the Philistines
  ruling his own people.
  He knew the Israelites
  wanted to be free.

"When I'm bigger,
  I'll teach those Philistines
  a lesson,"
  thought Samson.

But when he grew up,
  he fell in love
  with a Philistine girl.

"Please, Dad," said Samson,
  "I'd like to marry her."

Manoah didn't like the idea.

"There are hundreds
  of pretty girls
  among our own people, Son.
  Why not choose one of them?"

In the end his father agreed,
  and they all walked over
  to the girl's town.

Samson went on alone to meet her.

As he ran excitedly
  through the olive orchard,
  a young lion
  snarled and sprang at him.

Roarrrrrrr!

But suddenly
  Samson found he had
  ENORMOUS
  strength.

He managed to kill that lion
  with his bare hands!

On his way back from talking
  with his girlfriend,
  Samson noticed bees
  buzzing around
  the dead lion's body.

They had made their nest
  inside it!

Samson scooped out the honey
  and took it back
  to his mother and father,
  licking his fingers.

Then they went home
  to prepare for the wedding.

At his wedding
  Samson thought of a way
  to trick the Philistines.

"Listen, everyone," he shouted.
  "If you can answer my riddle,
  I'll make you rich. If you can't,
  you must make ME rich."

The Philistines were sure
  they would win, so they agreed.

"Out of the eater
  came something to eat;
  out of the strong
  came something sweet,"
  said Samson mysteriously.

Although the Philistines
  racked their brains,
  they just could not guess
  the answer.

(But you can, can't you?)

When harvest came,
  Samson thought of
  some more mischief to do.

He caught 300 foxes
  and set them loose
  in the wheat,
  with lighted torches
  between their tails.

Soon the wheat
  was on fire,
  with angry Philistines
  doing their best
  to put out the blaze.

They shook their fists at Samson.
  "Just you wait!" they yelled.

One day they saw him
  go into a house in Gaza.

"Now's our chance,"
  they whispered.
  "We'll close the city gates!"

But strong Samson
  just grabbed hold
  of the huge gates,
  pulled them up with
  posts, bars and all,
  and ran off up the hill
  with the gates
  on his shoulders.

The Philistines
  were hopping mad!

They promised money to a woman
  named Delilah if she could find out
  the secret of Samson's strength.

So Delilah fluttered
  her eyelashes and tried.
  "Samson, dear,
  please tell me what
  makes you so strong
  and what would take
  your strength away?"

Samson wasn't fooled.
  He decided
  to play some tricks
  on Delilah.

He told her
  he would lose his strength
  if he was bound with bow strings.

(But, of course, he got free easily!)

She nagged
  and nagged
  and nagged
  until at last
  Samson blurted out the truth.

"My strength is in my hair,
  if you really want to know.
  Now give me some peace!"

That night, as Samson slept,
  Delilah cut his hair.

The Philistines captured him
  and bound him up.

They also put out his eyes.
  Samson lost his sight
  as well as his strength.

Then he told her
  to weave his hair tightly
  and fix it to a loom with a pin.

(Of course, Samson just pulled
  out the pin and was free!)

He told her
  to have him bound
  with new ropes.

(But, of course, he snapped them
  like thread!)

But Delilah didn't give up.

The Philistines felt
  a lot safer
  with Samson weak.

Just to make sure,
  they chained him
  and made him grind corn
  at the prison mill.

But what they didn't notice
  was that Samson's hair
  began to grow!

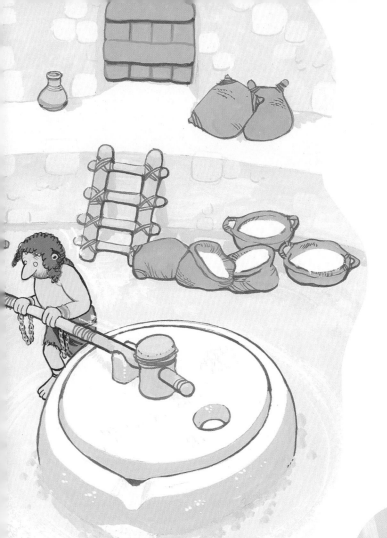

Using all his new strength
  he p-u-s-h-e-d
  those pillars HARD.

They cracked;
  they broke;
  and the whole building
  fell in with an
  earsplitting crrrash!

That was the end of Samson;
  and the end of
  those Philistines, too!

Note:
This story is found in Judges 13:2 – 16:31.

Soon after, the Philistines
  held a great feast.
  The hall was full of people
  drinking and eating.

"Let's have Samson up here
  so we can tease him!"
  suggested one man.

So Samson was led
  in to the feast.
  He stood between
  the two main pillars
  which held up the hall,
  and he had an idea.

David Meets Goliath

David was a very brave boy.
Even though he was small,
he wasn't afraid even of a great
big giant named Goliath.

Saul had been king of the Israelites
for a long, long time.

He had fought many battles
against those who did not believe
in the one true God.
— especially the Philistines.

God helped Saul and his people
in all their battles,
as long as they kept God's Word.

But then Saul
stopped listening to God,
and did not do what God asked.

He was no longer God's friend.

God looked elsewhere
for someone
who was truly His friend
to become king instead of Saul.

In the temple
there was a high priest,
a very holy man, named Samuel.

God told Samuel
to go to Bethlehem
and to call the family
of a man named Jesse
to join him in worship there.

Jesse came, with seven of his sons:
Eliab, Abinadab, Shammah
and four others.

"Haven't you got another son?"
Samuel asked Jesse.

"Well, yes," said Jesse,
"there's little David,
but he's so young
we left him
to look after the sheep."

"Send for him!" Samuel said.

And when David joined them,
God told Samuel that this
was the one He had chosen.

So Samuel took the holy oil,
  and poured it over David
  as a sign that God had chosen him
  to be His special servant.

One day David would be king.

Some time later
  the Philistines got ready
  for a new war against
  King Saul and his people.

King Saul gathered his army
  — which included
  David's brothers
  Eliab, Abinadab and Shammah —
  as fast as he could,
  and they marched off to meet
  the Philistine army.

The Philistines were ready
  on a hilltop near the border,
  so King Saul set his army
  on the hilltop across the valley
  from the Philistines.

Suddenly, Saul and his army
  saw something glistening
  in the valley.
  At first they thought it was
  a huge bronze statue,
  as big as a house!

What a fright they got
  when what they thought
  was a statue began to speak!
  It was a giant,
  dressed in bronze armor.

"My name is Goliath,"
 the giant shouted,
 "and I am the champion
 of the Philistines.

"Choose a champion,"
 Goliath the giant shouted
 to King Saul and the Israelites.
 "Send him out to meet me
 by himself!

"If he wins, and kills me,
 then the Philistines will surrender
 and you will have won.
 If I win, and kill your champion,
 then you must all surrender
 and be slaves of the Philistines."

Saul and his army were scared
 because they could find
 no champion to face Goliath.

The days went past,
 and each day Goliath made
 the same challenge,
 but still there was no one
 from King Saul's army
 to face him.

David's father was worried
 about his three sons in the army
 — they had gone off
 in such a hurry.
 He sent David to take them
 some extra food.

When David reached the army,
 he heard everyone talking
 about Goliath and his challenge.

"Do you mean to tell me,"
 David asked,
 "that not one of you
 has answered the challenge?"

"Listen, shrimp!"
 said David's oldest brother.
 (David really was so young
 and so very small.)
 "You get back to your sheep
 and leave the fighting
 to real men."

"Huh!" snorted David.
 "Real men would trust in
 the real God to save them.
 Goliath and his army don't
 believe in God, so God
 will help us defeat him.

"With God's help, even I
 could beat Goliath!"

This made the soldiers laugh —
   the very idea that a boy
   could face up to such
   a huge, strong giant!

It was such a joke around the camp
   that King Saul heard of it,
   and called David before him.

"You!" said Saul,
   when he saw
   how tiny David was.
   "Goliath could blow you over!"

David stood his ground
   and told King Saul
   how he protected
   his father's sheep
   from wild animals.

"God gave me strength
   against a lion
   and against a bear," David said,
   "and God will give me strength
   against this pagan giant."

"Oh, all right!" said Saul.
   "But you'd better take
   my armor."

But when David tried on
   Saul's armor,
   it was so big and
   he was so little that
   it just fell off again!

So David took his shepherd's stick,
   picked five small, smooth and round
   stones from the river bed,
   put them in his bag,
   and with his slingshot in his hand,
   went off to meet Goliath.

When Goliath saw
   how small David was,
   he began to shake with laughter.

David shouted across to him,
   "Laugh at me if you like,
   but do not laugh at
   the one true God
   who will help me
   to strike you down."

This story shows how
  God protects those
  who believe in Him
  and put their trust in Him.

Because David was a
  special friend of God,
  chosen by God and marked
  by the holy oil,
  he was able to defeat
  even a great giant.

Note:
This story is found
in 1 Samuel, chapters 16 and 17.

First Goliath and then David
  moved into the open space
  in the valley between the armies.

As Goliath came toward him,
  David took a stone from his bag,
  slung it and hit Goliath
  right in the middle
  of the forehead.

Goliath's knees crumpled,
  and crash!
  He fell on his face
  on the ground — dead!

King Saul and his army
  began to cheer
  and they chased
  the Philistine army away.

The Prophets' Competition

King Ahab believed in a false god named Baal. One day, God's prophet Elijah had a competition with Baal's prophets to prove that God, not Baal, is the true God.

About 100 years after the great
  King Solomon died,
  the people of Israel
  were ruled by King Ahab.

King Ahab married a foreign
  princess named Jezebel
  and made her his queen.

She did not believe
  in the one true God,
  but believed instead in a false god
  known as "Baal."

King Ahab loved Jezebel very much
  and would do anything
  to please her
  — even if it was wrong.

Just to please Jezebel,
  Ahab turned away
  from the one true God.
  He forgot all about his prayers.
  He even built a temple
  to the false Baal
  so that people
  could worship there.

God sent His prophet Elijah
  to give King Ahab and his people
  this message:

"God — the one true God —
  says this:
  'Because you have turned
  your backs on Me,
  I will turn My back on you.
  There will be no more rain
  until you turn again to Me.'"

In a hot land like Israel,
  the crops,
  the fruit trees
  and the grapes
  would all die without water.

Then the people and animals
  would starve.

Because Elijah brought
  such bad news,
  King Ahab and Queen Jezebel
  hated him.

Elijah had to go and hide
  in a cave in the mountains.

Queen Jezebel made King Ahab
  send soldiers out
  to look for Elijah —
  and anyone else who
  spoke up for the one true God —
  to capture them
  and to put them to death.

Three years passed,
  and still there was no rain.

Lots of the crops were dead.

Many of the animals,
  with nothing to eat or drink,
  were dying.

All of the people were
  thin, sick and sad.

In the third year,
  God told Elijah to go back
  and speak to King Ahab again.

You can imagine what kind of mood
  King Ahab was in!

"Why have you come back
  to annoy us?"
  the king shouted at Elijah.
  "Look at all the trouble
  you've caused
  — three years without rain!"

"It was not I who caused it,"
  said Elijah sternly,
  "but you!"
  (he pointed at King Ahab)
  "and you!"
  (he pointed at Queen Jezebel).

"You turned your back
  on the one true God
  and believed in this Baal
  nonsense!

"And I'll prove it's nonsense!
  Gather the people
  and all the priests of Baal
  and meet me on Mount Carmel
  — where there used to be an altar
  to the one true God,
  until you had it smashed down."

King Ahab sent his messengers out
  to tell everyone
  to gather on Mount Carmel.

They all came, wondering
  what was going to happen.

Everyone was there:
  King Ahab and Queen Jezebel,
  all the people,
  and more than 400 priests
  of the false god Baal.

Elijah stepped out
  in front of everyone.
  "Today," he said in a loud voice
  so that everyone could hear,
  "you must choose —
  either the false god"
  (he pointed to Baal's altar)
  "or the one true God"
  (he pointed to the ruins
  of God's altar).

No one said anything.

Elijah and all the people
watched them.

When everything was ready,
they started praying out loud
to Baal.
"Hear us, mighty Baal!"
they chanted,
and they began
their special strange dancing
around the altar.

"Send fire and take our sacrifice!"
they sang.

But nothing happened.

They kept on singing and dancing,
but by midday
still nothing had happened.

Elijah began to make fun of them:
"Maybe this god of yours
is asleep;
you'd better shout louder
to wake him up!"

They tried, but nothing happened.

Elijah started laughing.

"So then," said Elijah,
"I challenge the priests of Baal.
We'll both prepare a sacrifice,
but we will not light the bonfire.
You call on your gods,
and I will call on my God.
Whichever answers with fire
is God indeed!"

"Agreed!" the people shouted.

The priests of Baal started first.

Some put the wood on the altar,
while others took the bull
and made it ready for sacrifice.

Then Elijah asked the people
to soak the bonfire in water.
Three times they threw
jars of water all over it
till it was soaked
through and through
and the trench
was filled with water.

Who could light the bonfire now?

When everything was ready,
Elijah moved to the altar
and prayed:
"Lord God,
You are the one true God.
Let Your people see
that You are the one true God;
that You are their God,
and that we are Your people."

"Maybe your god is on
vacation!"

The priests of Baal kept trying
until evening came,
and they were all exhausted.

But nothing happened.

Then Elijah stepped forward.

He fixed up the altar of God
that had been smashed.

He dug a trench
right around the altar.
When the bull was ready,
he laid it on top of the wood
he had already placed there.

56

Elijah turned to King Ahab
  and said:
  "You can go home now,
  and prepare to eat and drink,
  because God will give you rain."

While King Ahab and the people
  made their way
  down the mountain,
  Elijah prayed for rain.
  And, do you know,
  the people were not even home
  before the sky was full
  of black clouds?

There was the most
  enormous thunderstorm
  and a really good downpour.

The plants, the animals,
  and the people
  could all drink, eat
  and live again!

Note:
This story is found
in 1 Kings 18:16 – 46.

Suddenly the fire fell onto the altar,
  burning fast and hot —
  so hot that it completely dried up
  all the water in the trench.

All the people were amazed,
  and fell on their knees, saying:
  "This indeed
  is the one true God!"

There and then
  they smashed the altar
  of the false god Baal,
  and got rid of his false priests.

Jonah and the Big Fish

Jonah tried to run away from God, but found that he couldn't. He then did God's work by teaching the people of Nineveh.

Jonah lived in Israel.

He was a prophet
  who taught the people
  God's messages and teachings.

But he didn't always do
  what God wanted him to do!

One day
  God gave Jonah a message
  — a warning —
  for the people of Nineveh
  in the land of Assyria.

Now Israel and Assyria
  were bitter enemies
  and the people of Nineveh
  were very wicked.

Do you think Jonah wanted to go
  to his enemies?

"No, I won't do it," he said.

"Yes, you will," said God.

"No, I won't," said Jonah,
  and he made up his mind
  to run away from God.

He boarded a boat about to sail
  out of Joppa Harbor
  to a far-off country.

"God won't find me there,"
  he thought smugly to himself.

By now Jonah was very tired
  and he went to sleep
  in the ship's hold.

While he was sleeping,
  a violent storm arose.

The sky was dark
  and the rain lashed down;
  thunder rolled
  and lightning flashed;
  and the huge waves
  crashed down on the decks.

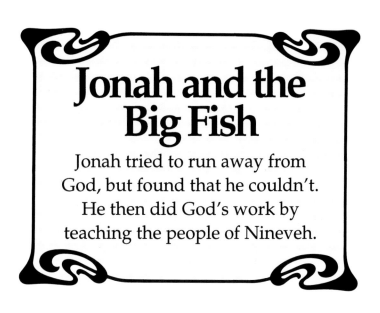

The sailors were terrified
  and prayed to their own gods
  of clay and bronze to save them.
  Then they threw their cargo
  overboard
  in order to lighten the load.

Still the storm raged.

And still Jonah slept...
  that is, until the captain saw him.
  "Hey!" shouted the captain
  above the storm.
  "Wake up, Jonah!
  We're going to draw straws.
  Whoever gets the shortest stick
  is to blame for this storm."

Guess who drew
  the shortest stick?
  Jonah!

Then Jonah realized that
  he could not run away
  from God.
  God is everywhere.

"Throw me overboard," said Jonah,
  "then God will stop the storm."

The sailors didn't want
  Jonah to drown.

But the storm got worse
  and worse
  and the boat was in danger
  of sinking.

So eventually they agreed
  and threw Jonah over the side...
  splash!
  And immediately
  the storm stopped.

When the sailors saw
  how powerful God is,
  they believed in Him
  and thanked Him
  for saving their lives.

But God had not forgotten Jonah.

Jonah tumbled through the
  water...
  down...
  down...
  down...
  he went; deeper...
  and deeper...
  until he fell into
  a huge, dark hole.

Guess where he was?
  Inside the tummy of
  the biggest fish
  you can imagine!

Jonah was sorry he had tried
  to run away from God
  and he thanked God
  for saving him.

After three days and nights
  the fish spat Jonah out
  onto a beach.

"Now, Jonah," said God,
  "go to Nineveh
  and give the people
  My warning."

"Yes, Lord," said Jonah, meekly,
  as he picked himself up
  off the beach.

He knew he must obey God now,
  and so he started
  on his journey to Nineveh.

Nineveh was a big city
  with many tall buildings.

Jonah was a little frightened,
  but he began to tell
  the people of God's warning:

"You must change
  your wicked ways
  and believe and obey God,
  otherwise this city
  will be destroyed
  in 40 days."

The people listened, and
strangely, they believed Jonah!

Even the king believed
  Jonah's warning.

He ordered everyone
  to turn from their wickedness
  and listen to God's teaching.
  All the people had to
  stop eating and drinking,
  and wear sackcloth
  and sit in ashes
  for a few days
  to show how sorry they were —
  including the king!

God made a plant grow up
  next to Jonah that night,
  and the leaves shielded him
  from the heat of the sun
  and the hot desert wind
  during the day.

Jonah was very pleased
  to have the shade of the plant.

But, the next day…

God sent a worm
  to attack the plant,
  and it shriveled up and died.

Jonah was left without any shelter
  from the blazing sun
  and the burning sting
  of the wind.

Jonah was angry
  that the plant had died —
  how thoughtless and selfish
  of the worm!

When God saw that the people
  of Nineveh
  were truly sorry
  and believed in Him,
  He forgave them
  and did not destroy their city.

This made Jonah very angry —
  he felt so foolish!

Poor Jonah.
  He never could learn.

"I knew You were a kind,
  loving God
  and would forgive them,"
  he moaned.
  "That's why I didn't want to go
  in the first place.
  They are our enemies."

He was so angry,
  he stalked off into the desert
  and sat and sulked in the hot sun.

So God decided to teach
  Jonah another lesson.

Then God said to Jonah:

"Why are you so angry, Jonah?
  This plant grew up one day
  and died the next day.
  You did nothing to make it grow
  but you feel sorry for it.
  Why should you care?"

Jonah shrugged his shoulders:
  "Well, it was useful to me."

"Hmmm," said God,
  "The plant is like
  the city of Nineveh.
  Isn't it better for Me
  to have pity on a city
  full of so many people?"

"I suppose so," said Jonah,
  kicking some stones.
  He felt kind of silly.

At last, Jonah understood
  and he was happy
  that God loved and cared
  so much
  about all people everywhere
  that He was willing
  to forgive them.

So he stopped sulking
  and started smiling
  and he began the journey
  back to Israel.

Note:
This story is found
in the book of Jonah.